L.O.V.E.

Interactive Workbook for Women

Resources by Les and Leslie Parrott
Books
Becoming Soul Mates
The Complete Guide to Marriage Mentoring
Getting Ready for the Wedding
I Love You More (and workbooks)*
Just the Two of Us
L.O.V.E. (and workbooks)*
Love Is . . .
The Love List
Love Talk (and workbooks)*
Meditations on Proverbs for Couples
*The Parent You Want to Be**
Pillow Talk
Questions Couples Ask
Relationships (and workbook)
Saving Your Marriage Before It Starts (and workbooks)*
Saving Your Second Marriage Before It Starts (and workbooks)*
Trading Places (and workbooks)*
Your Time-Starved Marriage (and workbooks)*
51 Creative Ideas for Marriage Mentors

Video Curriculum — ZondervanGroupware®
Complete Resource Kit for Marriage Mentoring
I Love You More
Love Talk
Saving Your Marriage Before It Starts

Books by Les Parrott
The Control Freak
*Crazy Good Sex**
Helping Your Struggling Teenager
High Maintenance Relationships
The Life You Want Your Kids to Live
Seven Secrets of a Healthy Dating Relationship
*Shoulda, Coulda, Woulda**
Once Upon a Family
*3 Seconds**
25 Ways to Win with People (coauthored with John Maxwell)
Love the Life You Live (coauthored with Neil Clark Warren)

Books by Leslie Parrott
*The First Drop of Rain**
If You Ever Needed Friends, It's Now
*You Matter More Than You Think**
God Loves You Nose to Toes (children's book)
Marshmallow Clouds (children's book)

•Audio version available

L.O.V.E.

Interactive Workbook for Women

Drs. Les & Leslie
PARROTT

ZONDERVAN.com/
AUTHORTRACKER
follow your favorite authors

ZONDERVAN

L.O.V.E. Interactive Workbook for Women
Copyright © 2010 by The Foundation for Healthy Relationships

Requests for information should be addressed to:

Zondervan, Grand Rapids, Michigan 49530

ISBN 978-0-310-327066

Published in association with Yates & Yates, www.yates2.com.

Interior design: Matthew Van Zomeren

Printed in the United States of America

09 10 11 12 13 14 15 • 22 21 20 19 18 17 16 15 14 13 12 11 10 9 8 7 6 5 4 3 2 1

CONTENTS

A Letter to Our Readers 7

Part One: Exploring Love Styles

Exploring Your Personality Masks 11

Pinpointing Your Love Style 17

Part Two: Exploring Your Love Style

Especially for the Leader: The Take-Charge Spouse. . . .25

Especially for the Optimist: The Encouraging Spouse . 35

Especially for the Validator: The Devoted Spouse. 45

Especially for the Evaluator: The Careful Spouse 55

Part Three: Exploring Your Spouse's Love Style

Especially for the Spouse of a Leader. 67

Especially for the Spouse of an Optimist 77

Especially for the Spouse of a Validator 87

Especially for the Spouse of an Evaluator. 97

**Part Four: For Group or Couple Discussion
with the Accompanying DVD**

Introduction 111

How Your Personality Shapes Your Marriage 113

What's a "Love Style"? 117

The Four Love Styles. 121

Putting Your Love Styles to Work for You 125

Appendix A: Comparing the Four Love Styles 129

*Appendix B: Exploring Your Online L.O.V.E.
Styles Report: An Exercise Kit for Couples* 131

A LETTER TO OUR READERS

WE'VE ALWAYS ENJOYED this quote from comedian Woody Allen: "I took a speed reading course and read *War and Peace* in twenty minutes. It involves Russia."

Ever felt like that after reading a book? We have. Sometimes it becomes so easy to focus on finishing a book that we miss its main message. What you hold in your hand is a kind of insurance policy against that happening while you are exploring *L.O.V.E.* But it's more than that, too.

Of course, we don't know you. But we know that you are unique—that nobody else on the planet is just like you. And we know the same holds true for your spouse. *L.O.V.E.* and the accompanying workbooks are designed to help you discover the unique combination of your two personalities and how they create a "Love Style" that will forever stand guard over your marriage.

Since you're working through these workbooks, we know you're eager to understand your own Love Style. Well, we've got a simple online assessment designed to help you do just that. The book talks more about this online assessment, but if you're already curious, you'll find it at www.RealRelationships.com. The Love Style Assessment takes less than ten minutes, and it provides you with twelve pages of personalized information on your unique way of giving and receiving love.

We have designed these workbooks—one for men and one for women—to help you incorporate into your relationship the new lessons you learn while reading. Of course, these workbooks are not required—they are simply options to help you take the content to a deeper and more personal level.

As you proceed through the pages of this workbook, make it your own. Don't get too hung up on following the rules. If a particular exercise leads you down a more intriguing path, take it. Some of these exercises may simply serve as springboards to discussions that fit your style more appropriately. However, if an exercise seems a bit challenging, don't give up on it. As the saying goes, anything worth having is worth working for—especially when it comes to our relationships.

So, whether you are a speed-reader or not, we hope you don't approach *L.O.V.E* just to check it off your "to-do" list. We hope and pray that you will, instead, use these exercises and discussion questions to internalize the book's message and fortify your relationship with a deep understanding of your unique Love Style.

Drs. Les and Leslie Parrott
Seattle, Washington

PART ONE

EXPLORING LOVE STYLES

WHATEVER YOUR PERSONAL style is, you'll want to begin with this section of the workbook. It will help you internalize the "big picture" as it relates to how and why the melding of your two personalities together is so valuable to understand. In other words, this introductory section will make the content of the book far more personal.

EXPLORING YOUR PERSONALITY MASKS

THE FIRST CHAPTER of the book points out that your marriage is one of a kind. Your relationship is unique. There's never been a couple just like you. So to get your wheels turning right from the outset, consider what makes your marriage distinctive.

Below is a diagram representing you and your husband. On the lines provided below, write three special qualities that are particularly noticeable in each of your personalities. Do this without consulting with your husband quite yet. Just note three positive qualities you possess and three that he possesses.

You

1. _____
2. _____
3. _____

Your Husband

1. _____
2. _____
3. _____

Your blended qualities

_____

_____

_____

Now, as you consider the six qualities you've noted above, think about how they combine to create something special that you don't see in other couples. Again, do this on your own, without consulting your husband. And take some time to think this through. What combination of personality traits combine to make your marriage unique? Jot your thoughts about this in the rectangle above.

Time to Talk #1

Once you have completed this section, ask your husband to offer you feedback on his perception of these special qualities. You can do the same for him once he has completed this section in his workbook.

The goal is simply to have a meaningful discussion about your uniqueness as a couple. Do your best to be open and receptive to his feedback—and be gracious and sensitive in your feedback to your husband.

You may want to jot a note or two on your discussion here:

The chapter also talks about how we all start out wearing "masks" in our relationship to create a positive impression of who we are for our eventual spouse. Our self-conscious efforts to win our partner's heart are natural. What masks did you wear in the early days of your dating relationship?

Just for fun, identify any and all masks you wore. Remember, these are not qualities you naturally have. These are qualities you tried to convey you had when you didn't really (because you thought they would be desirable to your date). In other words, these are masks you wore — that were not you — to give your eventual husband a more positive impression of you. Place a check mark next to each mask that applied to you in the early stages of your relationship.

The mask of being ...

☐ Goal-Oriented	☐ Fun-Loving	☐ Loyal	☐ Orderly
☐ Focused	☐ Positive	☐ Agreeable	☐ Conscientious
☐ Self-Confident	☐ Persuasive	☐ Thoughtful	☐ Scheduled
☐ Visionary	☐ Sociable	☐ Tolerant	☐ Purposeful
☐ Hardworking	☐ Encouraging	☐ Nurturing	☐ Factual
☐ Sensitive	☐ Authentic	☐ Extroverted	☐ Relaxed
☐ Easygoing	☐ Thick-Skinned	☐ Decisive	☐ Pleased
☐ Cool-Tempered	☐ Task-Oriented	☐ Adaptable	☐ Non-moody
☐ Agreeable	☐ On-Time	☐ Enthusiastic	☐ Trusting

We have a confession to make. Each one of these columns represents a cluster of traits from one of the four Love Styles that you'll read about in the next chapter (Leader, Optimist, Validator, and Evaluator). So which column has the most check marks for you? If one column seems to have more check marks than the others, that means you are likely to see that particular "style" as more desirable (or, at least, you used to).

Time to Talk #2

Once you have completed this section, ask your husband to offer you feedback on his perception of the masks you wore early on in your relationship. You can do the same for him once he has completed this section in his workbook.

The goal is to enjoy a meaningful conversation about how your real personalities, in their entirety, took a little while to truly reveal themselves. Enjoy some reminiscing and see what you can learn about yourself and why you wore the masks you did. Here are some questions to guide your conversation:

1. When and how did you first realize that I was wearing one of these masks?
2. What feelings did you have as you realized I was wearing a particular mask?
3. Do you think I'm still wearing masks in our marriage? If so, when and why?

You may want to jot a note or two on your discussion here:

You and the Five Domains of Real-Life Marriage

As you move into the next section of the book, you'll begin to see how your personal Love Style approaches the most common domains of your marriage. So, before you even learn about your own Love Style, it will be helpful for you to consider these domains and rate your current level of satisfaction with each.

On the following scales, note your general level of contentment with yourself—*not* with your husband—in each area.

1. Your Approach to Communication

Not Content							Very Content		
1	2	3	4	5	6	7	8	9	0

2. Your Approach to Conflict

Not Content							Very Content		
1	2	3	4	5	6	7	8	9	0

3. Your Approach to Sex and Intimacy

Not Content							Very Content		
1	2	3	4	5	6	7	8	9	0

4. Your Approach to Finances

Not Content							Very Content		
1	2	3	4	5	6	7	8	9	0

5. Your Approach to Free Time

Not Content							Very Content		
1	2	3	4	5	6	7	8	9	0

Once you have completed your rankings for yourself, go back to each of the five domains and indicate on the scales where you believe your husband would rank you. Be honest. And don't rank where you think your husband is, but how you believe he would rank you.

Time to Talk #3

Once you have completed this section, invite your husband into a discussion about it. You can do the same for him once he has completed this section in his workbook.

Talk about your self-perceptions in these domains and your perception of how he sees you in each one of them. Here are two sentence stems to jump-start your conversation with him:

1. The reason I marked this scale this way is because ...
2. The reason I thought you'd see me this way in this domain is because ...

Follow up by asking him what he thinks about your perceptions.

You may want to jot a note or two on your discussion here:

PINPOINTING YOUR LOVE STYLE

THIS CHAPTER INTRODUCES the concept of four fundamental personality groups by presenting you with two vitally important questions. When you accurately answer each of them, you'll have a pretty good idea of your fundamental L.O.V.E. Style:

L–Leader: The Take-Charge Spouse
O–Optimist: The Encouraging Spouse
V–Validator: The Devoted Spouse
E–Evaluator: The Careful Spouse

Let's take a more personal look at the two big questions that land you in one of the four categories.

Question #1: Are You Project-Oriented or People-Oriented?

As you read about this question in the book, how did you rank yourself on the following scale?

Project-Oriented						People-Oriented				
5	4	3	2	1	0	1	2	3	4	5

As you know, there is no right or wrong answer here. Fifty percent of the population falls into each side of this continuum—some people more extreme than others. Take a moment to list two or three immediate and concrete reasons why you placed yourself where you did on this measure:

Time to Talk #1

Once you have completed this brief section, ask your husband for feedback on it. You can do the same for him once he has completed this section in his workbook.

Ask him what he thinks of where you rated yourself. Does he agree with your rating? Why or why not? And does his opinion cause you to reconsider your ranking in either direction?

You may want to jot a note or two on your discussion here:

Question #2: Are You Fast-Paced or Slow-Paced?

Let's do the same for this second question. How did you rank yourself on the following scale?

Fast-Paced										Slow-Paced
5	4	3	2	1	0	1	2	3	4	5

Again, there are no right or wrong answers here. Once more, list two or three immediate and concrete reasons why you placed yourself where you did on this measure:

Time to Talk #2

Again, once you have completed this brief section, ask your husband for feedback on it. You can do the same for him once he has completed this section in his workbook.

Ask him what he thinks of where you rated yourself. Does he agree with your rating? Why or why not? And does his opinion cause you to reconsider your ranking in either direction?

You may want to jot a note or two on your discussion here:

With your self-ranking on these two scales, pinpoint where you land on the following graph. Place a mark on the spot that aligns with your rankings on each of the above continuums.

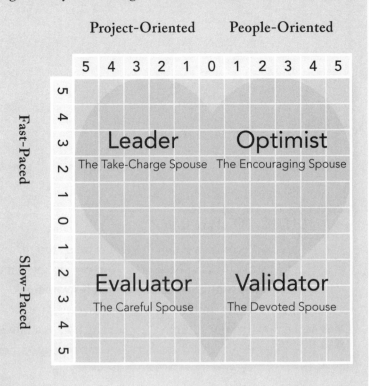

Once you have found your preliminary location on the graph (the online assessment will have you do this with more reliability, sophistication, and detail, if you choose to complete it), take a close look at the following table:

L O V E

	Leader: The Take-Charge Spouse	Optimist: The Encouraging Spouse	Validator: The Devoted Spouse	Evaluator: The Careful Spouse
Title				
Descriptor	Doer	Talker	Watcher	Thinker
Motivator	Power	Popularity	Peace	Perfection
Need	Control	Pleasure	Harmony	Excellence
Fear	Failure	Rejection	Conflict	Mediocrity
Satisfaction	Save Time	Win Approval	Gain Loyalty	Achieve Quality

How well do these one-word descriptions capture where you have placed yourself? Do the words under your column match you well? Why or why not? If you want to take this to a more elaborate level, you can use the more detailed table in Appendix A of this workbook.

The optional online Love Style Assessment will show you that you are likely a combination of one dominant category (L, O, V, or E) and a secondary category. At this point, do you identify with another column of words in this table? If so, which one and why?

Now, if you were to assign a percentage of your personality to each of the four categories in the chart where you have already pinpointed yourself, what would they be? Write the percentages here:

____% **L**–Leader: The Take-Charge Spouse
____% **O**–Optimist: The Encouraging Spouse
____% **V**–Validator: The Devoted Spouse
____% **E**–Evaluator: The Careful Spouse

PART TWO

EXPLORING YOUR
LOVE STYLE

IN THIS SECTION, we encourage you to go straight to the chapter of exercises devoted to your primary style (L, O, V, or E). Do that series of workbook exercises in that chapter first. Then, if you desire, go to the workbook chapter of exercises that represents your secondary style and complete them. There's no need for you to do all four of these exercise sets.

ESPECIALLY FOR THE LEADER: THE TAKE-CHARGE SPOUSE

THE FOLLOWING EXERCISES will help you drill down on some of the specific information you learned about your Love Style from the book. It will help you more carefully evaluate it for yourself. In addition, a major benefit to completing these brief exercises is the productive discussions you will have with your husband. In fact, you'll see that there are four clearly labeled "Time to Talk" portions where you will want to connect with your husband.

Feel free to complete all of the exercises in this workbook chapter before jumping into your conversations about what you're learning. Of course, you don't have to wait for the discussion at that specific point. It's up to you. But regardless of when you elect to do so, don't miss out on this major benefit. The discussions will pay big dividends in your relationship.

Your Deepest Needs

At the heart of every person's own Love Style are some deep-seated emotional needs that become instrumental in shaping one's behavior and attitudes. In other words, these deep needs become the motivation for much of what you do in your marriage relationship. And they are the key to unlocking what is so often mysterious to the husband who is not hardwired similarly.

In this section, we recommend that you consider how accurately these three needs describe what is going on beneath the surface of your personality. Simply circle the number on the scale to indicate the level of accuracy from your perspective:

Control: You like to have power and be in command. You feel good when you are at the proverbial reins.

Disagree									Agree
1	2	3	4	5	6	7	8	9	0

Efficiency and Speed: You live with a sense of urgency and want things to be done not only effectively but also quickly.

Disagree									Agree
1	2	3	4	5	6	7	8	9	0

Conformity: You want your husband to increase your productivity by getting onboard and not resisting your suggestions.

Disagree									Agree
1	2	3	4	5	6	7	8	9	0

Time to Talk #1

Once you have completed this section, ask your husband to offer you feedback on his perception of these three needs. You can do the same for him once he has completed this section in his workbook.

The goal is to simply have a meaningful discussion on your deepest needs. Do your best to be open and receptive to his feedback — and be gracious and sensitive in your feedback to your husband.

You may want to jot a note or two on your discussion here:

You at Your Best

As you know from the book, your specific Love Style generates several strengths. In this exercise we want you to order these five strengths we noted. Place a 1 next to the item that you think adds the *most value* to your marriage. Place a 2 next to the item that comes in second, and so on.

Use the first column of spaces (the second column will be used later for your husband to do the same thing):

You   Your Husband

—— ——   Goal-Oriented _____

—— ——   Focused _____

—— ——   Self-Confident _____

—— ——   Visionary _____

—— ——   Hardworking _____

Now, in the space to the right of each strength, note a specific example where you see this adding value to your marriage (for example, in your conversations, your finances, your love life, your free time, etc.).

You at Your Worst

Likewise, your specific Love Style generates some predictable areas of challenge. Order these five weaknesses. Place a 1 next to the item that you think is *most detrimental* to your marriage. Place a 2 next to the item that comes in second, and so on.

Use the first column of spaces (the second column will be used later for your husband to do the same thing):

You   Your Husband

—— ——   Stubborn _____

—— ——   Insensitive _____

—— ——   Easily Annoyed _____

—— ——   Hot-Tempered _____

—— ——   Domineering _____

Now, in the space to the right of each weakness, note a specific example where you see this being harmful to your marriage (for example, in your conversations, your finances, your love life, your free time, etc.).

Time to Talk #2

Once you have completed this section, ask your husband to do the same thing—for both your strengths and weaknesses. He can use the other column of spaces for this purpose. You can do the same for him once he has completed this section in his workbook.

The goal is to have a meaningful conversation about the perceptions you each have of what adds the most value to your relationship and what actually takes value away from it.

You may want to jot a note or two on your discussion here:

Your Definition of Love

The book provides the following definition of love that seems to fit many people with your Love Style. However, you might be inclined to edit this definition or add to it. Please do so in the space below:

**Love is ... being intentional and active
about building our future together.**

Based on your personal Love Style, what are two specific ways that you feel your husband could love you better in the next week?

1. _____

2. _____

You and the Five Domains of Real-Life Marriage

The book identifies how you approach some common issues in your marriage. Turn to that portion of the chapter if you need to review, and then complete the following five sentences with whatever comes to mind:

When it comes to communication, I ...

When it comes to conflict, I ...

When it comes to sex and intimacy, I ...

When it comes to finances, I ...

When it comes to free time, I ...

Time to Talk #3

Once you have completed this section, ask your husband to read through your sentence completions. For each one, discuss how your personal Love Style impacts this important domain of your relationship. Explore how your statements make him feel and ask him what he likes and dislikes about each one. You may also find it helpful to have him complete the sentences about you. In other words: "When it comes to communication, my wife ..." Of course, you can do the same thing for him once he completes this section of his workbook. By the way, be sure to keep a positive spirit and don't use this time to complain about each other.

You may want to jot a note or two on your discussion here:

How You Can Better Love Your Husband

The book suggests several ways that you may be able to better love your husband. In this section, consider each of them by noting *a specific example of how you might actually put it into practice*. If you can't think of any for a particular item, that's okay. Leave it blank and your husband may eventually have some suggestions.

You may want to refer back to this section of the book to jog your memory on these items:

Devise Some Marital Reminders
When, where, and how I can practice this:

Cultivate Patience
When, where, and how I can practice this:

Slow Down
When, where, and how I can practice this:

Put a Lid on Your Anger
When, where, and how I can practice this:

Lean into Grace
When, where, and how I can practice this:

Time to Talk #4

Once you have completed this section, ask your husband to read through your responses. Then ask him to talk through each one with you, noting how important it would be to him. As he does so, ask him for some concrete examples of when, where, and how he thinks that you could best practice this means of loving him. Of course, you can do the same thing for him once he completes this section of his workbook.

You may want to jot a note or two on your discussion here:

As you conclude this series of little exercises and conversations with your husband, we suggest that you note the most valuable personal insight or takeaway that you received in this process. Write it here:

ESPECIALLY FOR THE OPTIMIST: THE ENCOURAGING SPOUSE

THE FOLLOWING EXERCISES will help you drill down on some of the specific information you learned about your Love Style from the book. It will help you more carefully evaluate it for yourself. In addition, a major benefit to completing these brief exercises is the productive discussions you will have with your husband. In fact, you'll see that there are four clearly labeled "Time to Talk" portions where you will want to connect with your husband.

Of course, you don't have to wait for the discussion at that specific point. Feel free to complete all of the exercises in this workbook chapter before jumping into your conversations about what you're learning if you like. It's up to you. But, regardless of when you elect to do so, don't miss out on this major benefit. The discussions will pay big dividends in your relationship.

Your Deepest Needs

At the heart of every person's own Love Style are some deep-seated emotional needs that become instrumental in shaping one's behavior and attitudes. In other words, these deep needs become the motivation for much of what you do in your marriage relationship. And they are the key to unlocking what is so often mysterious to the husband who is not hardwired similarly.

In this section, we recommend that you consider how accurately these three needs describe what is going on beneath the surface of your personality. Simply circle the number on the scale to indicate the level of accuracy from your perspective:

Approval: You feed off of winning the acceptance of those around you—especially your husband. You thrive on compliments.

Disagree									Agree
1	2	3	4	5	6	7	8	9	0

Affection: You do everything you can to engender friend-ship and warm, heartfelt conversations.

Disagree									Agree
1	2	3	4	5	6	7	8	9	0

Fun: You are outgoing and cheerful. You like to laugh, joke, and entertain. You don't just go to a party, you are a party.

Disagree									Agree
1	2	3	4	5	6	7	8	9	0

Time to Talk #1

Once you have completed this section, ask your husband to offer you feedback on his perception of these three needs. You can do the same for him once he has completed this section in his workbook.

The goal is simply to have a meaningful discussion on your deepest needs. Do your best to be open and receptive to his feedback—and be gracious and sensitive in your feedback to your husband.

You may want to jot a note or two on your discussion here:

You at Your Best

As you know from the book, your specific Love Style generates several strengths. In this exercise we want you to order these five strengths we noted. Place a 1 next to the item that you think adds the *most value* to your marriage. Place a 2 next to the item that comes in second, and so on.

Use the first column of spaces (the second column will be used later for your husband to do the same thing):

You   Your
       Husband

—   —   Fun-loving _____

—   —   Positive _____

—   —   Persuasive _____

—   —   Sociable _____

—   —   Encouraging _____

Now, in the space to the right of each strength, note a specific example where you see this adding value to your marriage (for example, in your conversations, your finances, your love life, your free time, etc.).

You at Your Worst

Likewise, your specific Love Style generates some predictable areas of challenge. Order these five weaknesses. Place a 1 next to the item that you think is *most detrimental* to your marriage. Place a 2 next to the item that comes in second, and so on.

Use the first column of spaces (the second column will be used later for your husband to do the same thing):

You   Your
       Husband

—   —   Conflict Avoidant _____

—   —   Dramatic _____

—   —   Easily Distracted _____

—   —   Prone to Procrastinate _____

—   —   Forgetful _____

Now, in the space to the right of each weakness, note a specific example where you see this being harmful to your marriage (for example, in your conversations, your finances, your love life, your free time, etc.).

Time to Talk #2

Once you have completed this section, ask your husband to do the same thing—for both your strengths and weaknesses. He can use the other column of spaces for this purpose. You can do the same for him once he has completed this section in his workbook.

The goal is to have a meaningful conversation about the perceptions you each have of what adds the most value to your relationship and what actually takes value away from it.

You may want to jot a note or two on your discussion here:

Your Definition of Love

The book provides the following definition of love that seems to fit many people with your Love Style. However, you might be inclined to edit this definition or add to it. Please do so in the space below:

**Love is ... being fully attentive and giving
each other affection and acceptance.**

Based on your personal Love Style, what are two specific ways that you feel your husband could love you better in the next week?

1. _____

2. _____

You and the Five Domains of Real-Life Marriage

The book identifies how you approach some common issues in your marriage. Turn to that portion of the chapter if you need to review, and then complete the following five sentences with whatever comes to mind:

When it comes to communication, I ...

When it comes to conflict, I ...

When it comes to sex and intimacy, I ...

When it comes to finances, I ...

When it comes to free time, I . . .

Time to Talk #3

Once you have completed this section, ask your husband to read through your sentence completions. For each one, discuss how your personal Love Style impacts this important domain of your relationship. Explore how your statements make him feel and ask him what he likes and dislikes about each one. You may also find it helpful to have him complete the sentences about you. In other words: "When it comes to communication, my wife ..." Of course, you can do the same thing for him once he completes this section of his workbook. By the way, be sure to keep a positive spirit and don't use this time to complain about each other.

You may want to jot a note or two on your discussion here:

How You Can Better Love Your Husband

The book suggests several ways that you may be able to better love your husband. In this section, consider each of them by noting *a specific example of how you might actually put it into practice*. If you can't think of any for a particular item, that's okay. Leave it blank and your husband may eventually have some suggestions.

You may want to refer back to this section of the book to jog your memory on these items:

Be Willing to Disagree
When, where, and how I can practice this:

Shoot Straight
When, where, and how I can practice this:

Moderate Your Verbiage
When, where, and how I can practice this:

Respect the Plan
When, where, and how I can practice this:

Finish What You Start
When, where, and how I can practice this:

Time to Talk #4

Once you have completed this section, ask your husband to read through your responses. Then ask him to talk through each one with you, noting how important each would be to him. As he does so, ask him for some concrete examples of when, where, and how he thinks that you could best practice this means of loving him. Of course, you can do the same thing for him once he completes this section of his workbook.

You may want to jot a note or two on your discussion here:

As you conclude this series of little exercises and conversations with your husband, we suggest that you note the most valuable personal insight or takeaway that you received in this process. Write it here:

ESPECIALLY FOR THE VALIDATOR: THE DEVOTED SPOUSE

THE FOLLOWING EXERCISES will help you drill down on some of the specific information you learned about your Love Style from the book. It will help you more carefully evaluate it for yourself. In addition, a major benefit to completing these brief exercises is the productive discussions you will have with your husband. In fact, you'll see that there are four clearly labeled "Time to Talk" portions where you will want to connect with your husband.

Of course, you don't have to wait for the discussion at that specific point. Feel free to complete all of the exercises in this workbook chapter before jumping into your conversations about what you're learning if you like. It's up to you. But, regardless of when you elect to do so, don't miss out on this major benefit. The discussions will pay big dividends in your relationship.

Your Deepest Needs

At the heart of every person's own Love Style are some deep-seated emotional needs that become instrumental in shaping one's behavior and attitudes. In other words, these deep needs become the motivation for much of what you do in your marriage relationship. And they are the key to unlocking what is so often mysterious to the husband who is not hardwired similarly.

In this section, we recommend that you consider how accurately these three needs describe what is going on beneath the surface of your personality. Simply circle the number on the scale to indicate the level of accuracy from your perspective:

Harmony and Peace: You don't like confrontation or conflict. You do whatever you can to maintain agreement and union.

Disagree								Agree	
1	2	3	4	5	6	7	8	9	0

Stability: You like things to be consistent and steady. You love loyalty and don't like to make waves.

Disagree								Agree	
1	2	3	4	5	6	7	8	9	0

Esteem and Respect: You want your opinions acknowledged, respected, and heard—regardless of whether or not your husband agrees with you.

Disagree								Agree	
1	2	3	4	5	6	7	8	9	0

Time to Talk #1

Once you have completed this section, ask your husband to offer you feedback on his perception of these three needs. You can do the same for him once he has completed this section in his workbook.

The goal is simply to have a meaningful discussion on your deepest needs. Do your best to be open and receptive to his feedback—and be gracious and sensitive in your feedback to your husband.

You may want to jot a note or two on your discussion here:

You at Your Best

As you know from the book, your specific Love Style generates several strengths. In this exercise we want you to order these five strengths we noted. Place a 1 next to the item that you think adds *the most value* to your marriage. Place a 2 next to the item that comes in second, and so on.

Use the first column of spaces (the second column will be used later for your husband to do the same thing):

You   Your Husband

— — Loyal _____

— — Agreeable _____

— — Thoughtful _____

— — Tolerant _____

— — Nurturing _____

Now, in the space to the right of each strength, note a specific example where you see this adding value to your marriage (for example, in your conversations, your finances, your love life, your free time, etc.).

You at Your Worst

Likewise, your specific Love Style generates some predictable areas of challenge. Order these five weaknesses. Place a 1 next to the item that you think is *most detrimental* to your marriage. Place a 2 next to the item that comes in second, and so on.

Use the first column of spaces (the second column will be used later for your husband to do the same thing):

You   Your Husband

— — Introverted _____

— — Indecisive _____

— — Resistant to Change _____

— — Aloof _____

— — Unable to Say No _____

Now, in the space to the right of each weakness, note a specific example where you see this being harmful to your marriage (for example, in your conversations, your finances, your love life, your free time, etc.).

Time to Talk #2

Once you have completed this section, ask your husband to do the same thing—for both your strengths and weaknesses. He can use the other column of spaces for this purpose. You can do the same for him once he has completed this section in his workbook.

The goal is to have a meaningful conversation about the perceptions you each have of what adds the most value to your relationship and what actually takes value away from it.

You may want to jot a note or two on your discussion here:

Your Definition of Love

The book provides the following definition of love that seems to fit many people with your Love Style. However, you might be inclined to edit this definition or add to it. Please do so in the space below:

Love is ... being reassuring that we are on the same team and working together.

Based on your personal Love Style, what are two specific ways that you feel your husband could love you better in the next week?

1. _____

2. _____

You and the Five Domains of Real-Life Marriage

The book identifies how you approach some common issues in your marriage. Turn to that portion of the chapter if you need to review, and then complete the following five sentences with whatever comes to mind:

When it comes to communication, I ...

When it comes to conflict, I ...

When it comes to sex and intimacy, I ...

When it comes to finances, I ...

When it comes to free time, I ...

Time to Talk #3

Once you have completed this section, ask your husband to read through your sentence completions. For each one, discuss how your personal Love Style impacts this important domain of your relationship. Explore how your statements make him feel, and ask him what he likes and dislikes about each one. You may also find it helpful to have him complete the sentences about you. In other words: "When it comes to communication, my wife ..." Of course, you can do the same thing for him once he completes this section of his workbook. By the way, be sure to keep a positive spirit and don't use this time to complain about each other.

You may want to jot a note or two on your discussion here:

How You Can Better Love Your Husband

The book suggests several ways that you may be able to better love your husband. In this section, consider each of them by noting *a specific example of how you might actually put each into practice*. If you can't think of any for a particular item, that's okay. Leave it blank, and your husband may eventually have some suggestions.

You may want to refer back to this section of the book to jog your memory on these items:

Express Yourself
When, where, and how I can practice this:

Modify Your Plan
When, where, and how I can practice this:

Learn to Say No
When, where, and how I can practice this:

Join in the Excitement
When, where, and how I can practice this:

Share the Activity
When, where, and how I can practice this:

Time to Talk #4

Once you have completed this section, ask your husband to read through your responses. Then ask him to talk through each one with you, noting how important it would be to him. As he does so, ask him for some concrete examples of when, where, and how he thinks that you could best practice this means of loving him. Of course, you can do the same thing for him once he completes this section of his workbook.

You may want to jot a note or two on your discussion here:

As you conclude this series of little exercises and conversations with your husband, we suggest that you note the most valuable personal insight or takeaway that you received in this process. Write it here:

ESPECIALLY FOR THE EVALUATOR: THE CAREFUL SPOUSE

THE FOLLOWING EXERCISES will help you drill down on some of the specific information you learned about your Love Style from the book. It will help you more carefully evaluate it for yourself. In addition, a major benefit to completing these brief exercises is the productive discussions you will have with your husband. In fact, you'll see that there are four clearly labeled "Time to Talk" portions where you will want to connect with your husband.

Feel free to complete all of the exercises in this workbook chapter before jumping into your conversations about what you're learning. Of course, you don't have to wait for the discussion at that specific point. It's up to you. But, regardless of when you elect to do so, don't miss out on this major benefit. The discussions will pay big dividends in your relationship.

Your Deepest Needs

At the heart of every person's own Love Style are some deep-seated emotional needs that become instrumental in shaping one's behavior and attitudes. In other words, these deep needs become the motivation for much of what you do in your marriage relationship. And they are the key to unlocking what is so often mysterious to the husband who is not hardwired similarly.

In this section, we recommend that you consider how accurately these three needs describe what is going on beneath the surface of your personality. Simply circle the number on the scale to indicate the level of accuracy from your perspective:

Perfection: While not normally obtainable, you want to come as close as possible to perfection. You want to do things right and you want your efforts to be the best.

Disagree									Agree
1	2	3	4	5	6	7	8	9	0

Evaluative: You take the time to appraise each possibility. You ask probing questions and take notes in order to weigh the pros and cons.

Disagree									Agree
1	2	3	4	5	6	7	8	9	0

Quality: You aspire to excellence — you won't settle for mediocrity. You want your days to be of value and worth. You want them to count.

Disagree									Agree
1	2	3	4	5	6	7	8	9	0

Time to Talk #1

Once you have completed this section, ask your husband to offer you feedback on his perception of these three needs. You can do the same for him once he has completed this section in his workbook.

The goal is to simply have a meaningful discussion on your deepest needs. Do your best to be open and receptive to his feedback—and be gracious and sensitive in your feedback to your husband.

You may want to jot a note or two on your discussion here:

You at Your Best

As you know from the book, your specific Love Style generates several strengths. In this exercise we want you to order these five strengths we noted. Place a 1 next to the item that you think adds *the most value* to your marriage. Place a 2 next to the item that comes in second, and so on.

Use the first column of spaces (the second column will be used later for your husband to do the same thing):

You   Your
       Husband

—   —   Orderly _____

—   —   Conscientious _____

—   —   Scheduled _____

—   —   Purposeful _____

—   —   Factual _____

Now, in the space to the right of each strength, note a specific example where you see this adding value to your marriage (for example, in your conversations, your finances, your love life, your free time, etc.).

You at Your Worst

Likewise, your specific Love Style generates some predictable areas of challenge. Order these five weaknesses. Place a 1 next to the item that you think is *most detrimental* to your marriage. Place a 2 next to the item that comes in second, and so on.

Use the first column of spaces (the second column will be used later for your husband to do the same thing):

You   Your
       Husband

—   —   Obsessive _____

—   —   Critical _____

—   —   Moody _____

—   —   Suspicious _____

—   —   Rigid _____

Now, in the space to the right of each weakness, note a specific example where you see this being harmful to your marriage (for example, in your conversations, your finances, your love life, your free time, etc.).

Time to Talk #2

Once you have completed this section, ask your husband to do the same thing—for both your strengths and weaknesses. He can use the other column of spaces for this purpose. You can do the same for him once he has completed this section in his workbook.

The goal is to have a meaningful conversation about the perceptions you each have of what adds the most value to your relationship and what actually takes value away from it.

You may want to jot a note or two on your discussion here:

Your Definition of Love

The book provides the following definition of love that seems to fit many people with your Love Style. However, you might be inclined to edit this definition or add to it. Please do so in the space below:

Love is... being thorough, accurate, and true to our commitments and standards.

Based on your personal Love Style, what are two specific ways that you feel your husband could love you better in the next week?

1. _____

2. _____

You and the Five Domains of Real-Life Marriage

The book identifies how you approach some common issues in your marriage. Turn to that portion of the chapter if you need to review, and then complete the following five sentences with whatever comes to mind:

When it comes to communication, I ...

When it comes to conflict, I ...

When it comes to sex and intimacy, I ...

When it comes to finances, I ...

When it comes to free time, I . . .

Time to Talk #3

Once you have completed this section, ask your husband to read through your sentence completions. For each one, discuss how your personal Love Style impacts this important domain of your relationship. Explore how your statements make him feel and ask him what he likes and dislikes about each one. You may also find it helpful to have him complete the sentences about you. In other words: "When it comes to communication, my wife ..." Of course, you can do the same thing for him once he completes this section of his workbook. By the way, be sure to keep a positive spirit and don't use this time to complain about each other.

You may want to jot a note or two on your discussion here:

How You Can Better Love Your Husband

The book suggests several ways that you may be able to better love your husband. In this section, consider each of them by noting *a specific example of how you might actually put it into practice.* If you can't think of any for a particular item, that's okay. Leave it blank and your husband may eventually have some suggestions.

You may want to refer back to this section of the book to jog your memory on these items:

Lighten Up
When, where, and how I can practice this:

Relax the Rules
When, where, and how I can practice this:

Excuse the Incorrect Details
When, where, and how I can practice this:

Allow for Interruptions
When, where, and how I can practice this:

Power Down the Criticism
When, where, and how I can practice this:

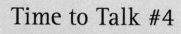

Time to Talk #4

Once you have completed this section, ask your husband to read through your responses. Then ask him to talk through each one with you, noting how important each would be to him. As he does so, ask him for some concrete examples of when, where, and how he thinks that you could best practice this means of loving him. Of course, you can do the same thing for him once he completes this section of her workbook.

You may want to jot a note or two on your discussion here:

As you conclude this series of little exercises and conversations with your husband, we suggest that you note the most valuable personal insight or takeaway that you received in this process. Write it here:

PART THREE

EXPLORING YOUR SPOUSE'S LOVE STYLE

IN THIS SECTION, we encourage you to once again go straight to the chapter of exercises devoted to the style (L, O, V, or E) that pertains to your marriage. Do the series of workbook exercises in that chapter first. Then, if you desire, go to the workbook chapter of exercises that represents the secondary style of your husband and complete them. There's no need for you to do all four of these exercise sets.

ESPECIALLY FOR THE SPOUSE OF A LEADER

WITH YOUR NEW understanding of your husband's Love Style, you have an opportunity to love him like you never have before. The following exercises will show you how.

As in the previous section of this workbook, you'll see that there are three clearly labeled "Time to Talk" portions where you will want to connect with your husband on various topics. And, of course, you don't have to wait for the discussion at that specific point. Feel free to complete all of the exercises in this workbook chapter before jumping into your conversations about what you're learning if you like. It's up to you.

What Your Husband Wants Most

In this brief exercise we help you serve up some "Desire Pie." The following desires are typically associated with your husband's "take charge" Love Style. Of course, some are more important to him than others. If you need a reminder on the details of each of these needs, you may want to review this portion in the book.

On the next page is an abbreviated summary of his likely desires. As you read each one, try your best to think of a recent and specific example (big or small) that represents this desire within him.

For example, when it comes to his desire for "agreement," maybe he got frustrated when you resisted an alternative choice for dinner last week. And when it comes to "facts," maybe he skips over describing his emotions about a dramatic change at work. You get the idea. Here you go:

Agreement and deference:
Specific example:

Facts more than feelings:
Specific example:

Support of his plan:
Specific example:

Anything that saves time:
Specific example:

Direct communication (to the point):
Specific example:

Logic and objectivity:
Specific example:

Competition (in playing games):
Specific example:

Before asking your husband to weigh in, try to determine how important each one of these seven desires is to him by assigning it a "slice" of the following pie chart. In the first circle, draw "slices" of the pie that represent the relative importance of these. You can give them a specific percentage if you like. Of course, some slices may be equal in size. And some may be a mere sliver. That's up to you.

So, do your best. Give this pie seven slices of varying sizes to represent your perception of your husband's deepest desires of what he wants most from you (labeling each slice):

Desire Pie

How You Perceive Your Husband's Desires

Now, in your "Time to Talk," your husband will use this second pie by slicing it up the way he sees the importance of each of the same seven desires himself.

Desire Pie

How Your Husband Perceives His Desires

Time to Talk #1

Once you have completed this section, ask your husband to slice up her "Desire Pie" in the second pie provided above. You can do the same for him once he has completed this section in his workbook. Once he has completed this, here are some questions to explore together:

1. What differences in perception do we have regarding your desires? Why do we have them?
2. How do we perceive your desires in the same ways? And what recent and specific examples led us to this?

Ask your husband: Which of your desires would you like me to focus on meeting the most? What suggestions do you have for me on how better to meet them?

As always, the goal is to have a meaningful discussion. Do your best to be open and receptive to his feedback—and be gracious and sensitive in your feedback to him.

You may want to jot a note or two on your discussion here:

How to Love Your Take-Charge Husband

The book makes several suggestions on how you can better love your husband. Below is a list of these. If you need a reminder on the details of each of these needs, you may want to review this portion in the book.

There are two easy steps to this little exercise. First, place a 1 next to the item that you think is *most important* to loving your husband. Place a 2 next to the item that comes in second, and so on. Use the first column of spaces (the second column will be used later for your husband to do the same thing):

You   Your Husband

___   ___   Get on Board or Get Out of the Way ___

___   ___   Look Beneath the Surface ___

___   ___   Concede When You Can ___

___   ___   Make His Life Easier ___

___   ___   Confirm the Complaints ___

___   ___   Understand the Gender Difference ___

___   ___   Praise Liberally ___

Now, in the space to the right of each suggestion, rank how realistic it is for you to practice each of these. That is, how likely are you to do this?

Not Realistic				**Very Realistic**
1	2	3	4	5

Which one is easiest for you to do for your husband? Why?

Which one is toughest for you to do for your husband? Why?

Time to Talk #2

After you have completed this section, ask your husband to use the second column to rank the importance of these items to him. You can do the same for him once he has completed this section in his workbook. Once he has completed this, here are some questions to explore together:

1. Do you agree on which behaviors are most important? If there is a discrepancy between the two of you on this, how do you account for it?
2. Discuss the best time to do each of these loving things. In other words, at what specific times is each one important? Be specific and use examples.
3. Talk about why some seem more realistic for you to do than others. Ask your husband what suggestions he has for you on any of these.

As always, the goal is to have a meaningful discussion. Be open and receptive to his feedback—and be gracious and sensitive in your feedback to him.

You may want to jot a note or two on your discussion here:

How to Stay Healthy with a Take-Charge Spouse

Your marriage can only be as healthy as the least healthy partner in it. To insure that you are doing your part to be emotionally healthy, review the qualities suggested in the book that you continue to work on.

Below are four thermometers, each one representing one of the qualities. If you were to measure how well you are doing at each one, what would the thermometer reading be? Draw a line at the appropriate place on each one to indicate this:

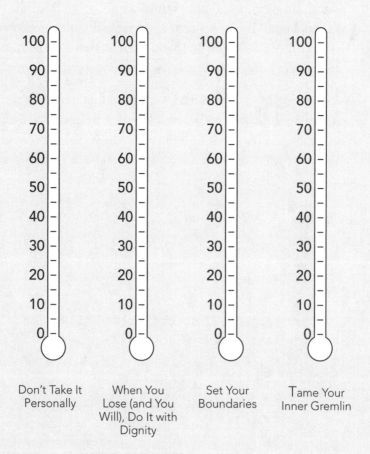

Don't Take It Personally

When You Lose (and You Will), Do It with Dignity

Set Your Boundaries

Tame Your Inner Gremlin

Of the four qualities, which one do you think is most important to work on right now in your life? Describe in specific terms one action you can take this week to do just that:

Time to Talk #3

Once you have completed this section, review it with your husband. Here are a couple of questions to guide your conversation, questions you can pose to him and discuss:

1. Do you agree that these are important things for me to do? Why or why not? Which one do you feel is most important (and least important) for me to do? Why?
2. Knowing that it's ultimately up to me, what is one practical and specific way that you can help me practice this kind of self-care?

You can answer the same questions for him once he completes his exercise in his workbook.

You may want to jot a note or two on your discussion here:

ESPECIALLY FOR THE SPOUSE OF AN OPTIMIST

WITH YOUR NEW understanding of your husband's Love Style, you have an opportunity to love him like you never have before. The following exercises will show you how.

As in the previous section of this workbook, you'll see that there are three clearly labeled "Time to Talk" portions where you will want to connect with your husband on various topics. And, of course, you don't have to wait for the discussion at that specific point. Feel free to complete all of the exercises in this workbook chapter before jumping into your conversations about what you're learning if you like. It's up to you.

What Your Husband Wants Most

In this brief exercise, we help you serve up some "Desire Pie." The following desires are typically associated with your husband's "encouraging" Love Style. Of course, some are more important to him than others. If you need a reminder on the details of each of these needs, you may want to review this portion in the book.

On the next page is an abbreviated summary of his likely desires. As you read each one, try your best to think of a recent and specific example (big or small) that represents this desire within him.

For example, when it comes to his desire for "a listening ear," maybe he got his feelings hurt when you seemed distracted by your cell phone while in a conversation with him. And when it comes to "sincere compliments," maybe he kept wearing that outfit you said you liked. You get the idea. Here you go:

A loving and listening ear:
Specific example of how you see this desire coming through in him:

Sincere compliments:
Specific example:

Laughter and fun:
Specific example:

Room to be spontaneous (not pinned down):
Specific example:

A chance to speak:
Specific example:

Unconditional acceptance:

Specific example:

Before asking your husband to weigh in, try to determine how important each one of these six desires is to him by assigning it a "slice" of the following pie chart. In the first circle, draw "slices" of the pie that represent the relative importance of these. You can give them a specific percentage if you like. Of course, some slices may be equal in size. And some may be a mere sliver. That's up to you.

So, do your best. Give this pie six slices of varying sizes to represent your perception of your husband's deepest desires of what he wants most from you (labeling each slice):

Desire Pie

How You Perceive Your Husband's Desires

Now, in your "Time to Talk," your husband will use this second pie by slicing it up the way he sees the importance of each of the same six desires himself.

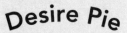

Desire Pie

How Your Husband Perceives His Desires

Time to Talk #1

Once you have completed this section, ask your husband to slice up him "Desire Pie" in the second pie provided above. You can do the same for him once he has completed this section in his workbook. Once he has completed this, here are some questions to explore together:

1. What differences in perception do we have regarding your desires? Why do we have them?
2. How do we perceive your desires in the same way? And what recent and specific examples led us to this?

3. Ask your husband: Which of your desires would you like me to focus on meeting the most? What suggestions do you have for me on how better to meet them?

As always, the goal is to have a meaningful discussion. Do your best to be open and receptive to his feedback—and be gracious and sensitive in your feedback to him.

You may want to jot a note or two on your discussion here:

How to Love Your Encouraging Husband

The book makes several suggestions on how you can better love your husband. Below is a list of these. If you need a reminder on the details of each of these needs, you may want to review this portion in the book.

There are two easy steps to this little exercise. First, place a 1 next to the item that you think is *most important* to loving your husband. Place a 2 next to the item that comes in second, and so on. Use the first column of spaces (the second column will be used later for your husband to do the same thing):

You Your Husband

___ ___   Affirm Liberally ___

___ ___   Be More Spontaneous ___

___ ___   Share the Troubles ___

___ ___   Clarify Their Details ___

___ ___   Ask for Honesty ___

___ ___   Show More Affection ___

___ ___   Flex on the Schedule ___

Now, in the space to the right of each suggestion, rank how realistic it is for you to practice each of these. That is, how likely are you to do this?

Not Realistic				Very Realistic
1	2	3	4	5

Which one is easiest for you to do for your husband? Why?

Which one is toughest for you to do for your husband? Why?

Time to Talk #2

Once you have completed this section, ask your husband to use the second column to rank the importance of these items to him. You can do the same for him once he has completed this section in his workbook. Once he has completed this, here are some questions to explore together:

1. Do you agree on which behaviors are most important? If there is a discrepancy between the two of you on this, how do you account for it?
2. Discuss the best time to do each of these loving things. In other words, at what specific times is each one important? Be specific and use examples.
3. Talk about why some seem more realistic for you to do than others. Ask your husband what suggestions he has for you on any of these.

As always, the goal is to have a meaningful discussion. Be open and receptive to his feedback—and be gracious and sensitive in your feedback to him.

You may want to jot a note or two on your discussion here:

How to Stay Healthy with an Encouraging Spouse

Your marriage can only be as healthy as the least healthy partner in it. To insure that you are doing your part to be emotionally healthy, review the qualities suggested in the book that you continue to work on.

Below are four thermometers, each one representing one of the qualities. If you were to measure how well you are doing at each one, what would the thermometer reading be? Draw a line at the appropriate place on each one to indicate this:

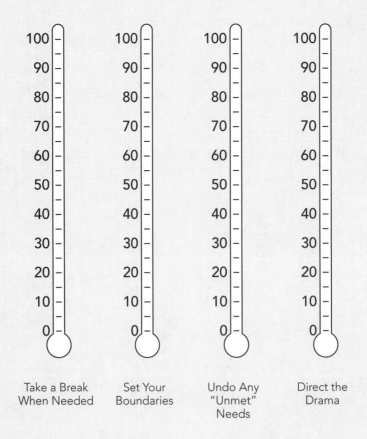

| Take a Break When Needed | Set Your Boundaries | Undo Any "Unmet" Needs | Direct the Drama |

Of the four qualities, which one do you think is most important to work on right now in your life? Describe in specific terms one action you can take this week to do just that:

Time to Talk #3

Once you have completed this section, review it with your husband. Here are a couple of questions to guide your conversation, questions you can pose to him and discuss:

1. Do you agree that these are important things for me to do? Why or why not? Which one do you feel is most important (and least important) for me to do and why?
2. Knowing that it's ultimately up to me, what is one practical and specific way that you can help me practice this kind of self-care?

You can answer the same questions for him once he completes his exercise in his workbook.

You may want to jot a note or two on your discussion here:

ESPECIALLY FOR THE SPOUSE OF A VALIDATOR

WITH YOUR NEW understanding of your husband's Love Style, you have an opportunity to love him like you never have before. The following exercises will show you how.

As in the previous section of this workbook, you'll see that there are three clearly labeled "Time to Talk" portions where you will want to connect with your husband on various topics. And, of course, you don't have to wait for the discussion at that specific point. Feel free to complete all of the exercises in this workbook chapter before jumping into your conversations about what you're learning if you like. It's up to you.

What Your Husband Wants Most

In this brief exercise we help you serve up some "Desire Pie." The following desires are typically associated with your husband's "Devoted" Love Style. Of course, some are more important to him than others. If you need a reminder on the details of each of these needs, you may want to review this portion in the book.

On the next page is an abbreviated summary of his likely desires. As you read each one, try your best to think of a recent and specific example (big or small) that represents this desire within him.

For example, when it comes to his desire for "a calm presence," maybe he gets flustered when you express anxiety or anger. And when it comes to "courtesy and patience," maybe he shuts down or pulls away emotionally when you try to rush him. You get the idea. Here you go:

A calm presence:
Specific example of how you see this desire coming through in him:

Courtesy and patience:
Specific example:

Unrushed time with you:
Specific example:

Advance warning of change:
Specific example:

Time to reflect:
Specific example:

Trust and meaning:
Specific example:

Before asking your husband to weigh in, try to deter-mine how important each one of these six desires is to him by assigning it a "slice" of the following pie chart. In the first circle, draw "slices" of the pie that represent the relative importance of these. You can give them a specific percentage if you like. Of course, some slices may be equal in size. And some may be a mere sliver. That's up to you.

So, do your best. Give this pie six slices of varying sizes to represent your perception of your husband's deepest desires of what he wants most from you (labeling each slice):

Desire Pie

How You Perceive Your Husband's Desires

Now, in your "Time to Talk," your husband will use this second pie by slicing it up the way he sees the importance of each of the same six desires himself.

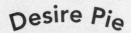

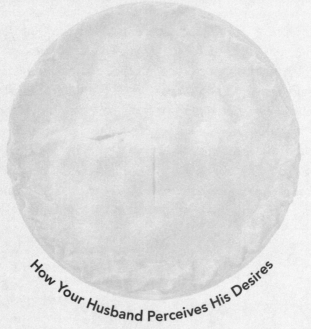

Time to Talk #1

Once you have completed this section, ask your husband to slice up his "Desire Pie" in the second pie provided above. You can do the same for him once he has completed this section in his workbook. Once he has completed this, here are some questions to explore together:

1. What differences in perception do we have regarding your desires? Why do we have them?
2. How do we perceive your desires in the same way? What recent and specific examples led us to this?

3. Ask your husband: Which of your desires would you like me to focus on meeting the most? What suggestions do you have for me on how better to meet them?

As always, the goal is to have a meaningful discussion. Do your best to be open and receptive to his feedback—and be gracious and sensitive in your feedback to him.

You may want to jot a note or two on your discussion here:

How to Love Your Devoted Husband

The book makes several suggestions on how you can better love your husband. Below is a list of these. If you need a reminder on the details of each of these needs, you may want to review this portion in the book.

There are two easy steps to this little exercise. First, place a 1 next to the item that you think is *most important* to loving your husband. Place a 2 next to the item that comes in second, and so on. Use the first column of spaces (the second column will be used later for your husband to do the same thing):

You   Your
        Husband

——   ——   Cultivate Significance ——

——   ——   Provide Warning of Change ——

——   ——   Provide Time for Adjustment ——

——   ——   Stay Calm ——

——   ——   Give Your Time ——

——   ——   Don't Push or Pressure ——

——   ——   Recognize Your Husband's Contribution ——

Now, in the space to the right of each suggestion, rank how realistic it is for you to practice each of these. That is, how likely are you to do this?

Not Realistic				**Very Realistic**
1	2	3	4	5

Which one is easiest for you to do for your husband? Why?

Which one is toughest for you to do for your husband? Why?

Time to Talk #2

Once you have completed this section, ask your husband to use the second column to rank the importance of these items to him. You can do the same for him once he has completed this section in his workbook. Once he has completed this, here are some questions to explore together:

1. Do you agree on which behaviors are most important? If there is a discrepancy between the two of you on this, how do you account for it?
2. Discuss the best time to do each of these loving things. In other words, at what specific time is each one important? Use examples.
3. Talk about why some seem more realistic for you to do than others. Ask your husband what suggestions he has for you on any of these.

As always, the goal is to have a meaningful discussion. Be open and receptive to his feedback—and be gracious and sensitive in your feedback to him.

You may want to jot a note or two on your discussion here:

How to Stay Healthy with a Devoted Spouse

Your marriage can only be as healthy as the least healthy partner in it. To insure that you are doing your part to be emotionally healthy, review the qualities suggested in the book that you continue to work on.

Below are four thermometers, each one representing one of the qualities. If you were to measure how well you are doing at each one, what would the thermometer reading be? Draw a line at the appropriate place on each one to indicate this:

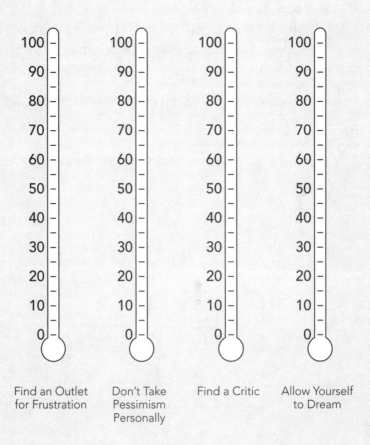

Find an Outlet for Frustration   Don't Take Pessimism Personally   Find a Critic   Allow Yourself to Dream

Of the four qualities, which one do you think is most important to work on right now in your life? Describe in specific terms one action you can take this week to do just that:

Time to Talk #3

Once you have completed this section, review it with your husband. Here are a couple of questions to guide your conversation, questions you can pose to him and discuss:

1. Do you agree that these are important things for me to do? Why or why not? Which one do you feel is most important (and least important) for me to do and why?
2. Knowing that it's ultimately up to me, what is one practical and specific way that you can help me practice this kind of self-care?

You can answer the same questions for him once he completes his exercise in his workbook.

You may want to jot a note or two on your discussion here:

ESPECIALLY FOR THE SPOUSE OF AN EVALUATOR

WITH YOUR NEW understanding of your husband's Love Style, you have an opportunity to love him like you never have before. The following exercises will show you how.

As in the previous section of this workbook, you'll see that there are three clearly labeled "Time to Talk" portions where you will want to connect with your husband on various topics. And, of course, you don't have to wait for the discussion at that specific point. Feel free to complete all of the exercises in this workbook chapter before jumping into your conversations about what you're learning if you like. It's up to you.

What Your Husband Wants Most

In this brief exercise, we help you serve up some "Desire Pie." The following desires are typically associated with your husband's "Careful" Love Style. Of course, some are more important to him than others. If you need a reminder of the details of each of these needs, you may want to review this portion in the book.

On the next page is an abbreviated summary of your husband's likely desires. As you read each one, try your best to *think of a recent and specific example (big or small)* that represents this desire within him.

For example, when it comes to his desire for lots of clear information, maybe he feels panicky when you make plans without detailed info. And when it comes to respecting space, maybe he gets angry when you borrow something from his desk without returning it. You get the idea. Here you go:

Lots of clear, detailed information:
Specific example of how you see this desire coming through inhim:

Respect for his space:
Specific example:

Time to do things right:
Specific example:

Appreciation of his efforts:
Specific example:

Time to think:
Specific example:

Justification of any deviation from the norm:
Specific example:

Before asking your husband to weigh in, try to determine how important each one of these six desires is to him by assigning it a "slice" of the following pie chart. In the first circle, draw "slices" of the pie that represent the relative importance of these. You can give them a specific percentage if you like. Of course, some slices may be equal in size. And some may be a mere sliver. That's up to you.

So, do your best. Give this pie six slices of varying sizes to represent your perception of your husband's deepest desires of what he wants most from you (labeling each slice):

Desire Pie

How You Perceive Your Husband's Desires

Now, in your "Time to Talk," your husband will use this second pie by slicing it up the way he sees the importance of each of the same six desires himself.

Desire Pie

How Your Husband Perceives His Desires

Time to Talk #1

Once you have completed this section, ask your husband to slice up his "Desire Pie" in the second pie provided above. You can do the same for him once he has completed this section in his workbook. Once he has completed this, here are some questions to explore together:

1. What differences in perception do we have regarding your desires? Why do we have them?
2. How do we perceive your desires in the same way? What recent and specific examples led us to this?

3. Ask your husband: Which of your desires would you like me to focus on meeting the most? What suggestions do you have for me on how to better meet them?

As always, the goal is to have a meaningful discussion. Do your best to be open and receptive to his feedback—and be gracious and sensitive in your feedback to him.

You may want to jot a note or two on your discussion here:

How to Love Your Careful Husband

The book makes several suggestions on how you can better love your husband. Below is a list of these. If you need a reminder on the details of each of these needs, you may want to review this portion in the book.

There are two easy steps to this little exercise. First, place a 1 next to the item that you think is *most important* to loving your husband. Place a 2 next to the item that comes in second, and so on. Use the first column of spaces (the second column will be used later for your husband to do the same thing):

You   Your
       Husband

——   ——   Do What You Say You're Going to Do ——

——   ——   Provide Stability ——

——   ——   Stroke the Ego and Don't Make Fun ——

——   ——   Provide Space and Quiet ——

——   ——   Keep Your Marriage Thank-Tank Full ——

Now, in the space to the right of each suggestion, rank how realistic it is for you to practice each of these. That is, how likely are you to do this?

Not Realistic				**Very Realistic**
1	2	3	4	5

Which one is easiest for you to do for your husband? Why?

Which one is toughest for you to do for your husband? Why?

Time to Talk #2

Once you have completed this section, ask your husband to use the second column to rank the importance of these items to him. You can do the same for him once he has completed this section in his workbook. Once he has completed this, here are some questions to explore together:

1. Do you agree on which behaviors are most important? If there is a discrepancy between the two of you on this, how do you account for it?
2. Discuss the best time to do each of these loving things. In other words, at what specific times is each one important? Use examples.
3. Talk about why some seem more realistic for you to do than others. Ask your husband what suggestions he has for you on any of these.

As always, the goal is to have a meaningful discussion. Be open and receptive to his feedback—and be gracious and sensitive in your feedback to him.

You may want to jot a note or two on your discussion here:

How to Stay Healthy with a Careful Spouse

Your marriage can only be as healthy as the least healthy partner in it. To insure that you are doing your part to be emotionally healthy, review the qualities suggested in the book that you continue to work on.

Below are four thermometers, each one representing one of the qualities. If you were to measure how well you are doing at each one, what would the thermometer reading be? Draw a line at the appropriate place on each one to indicate this:

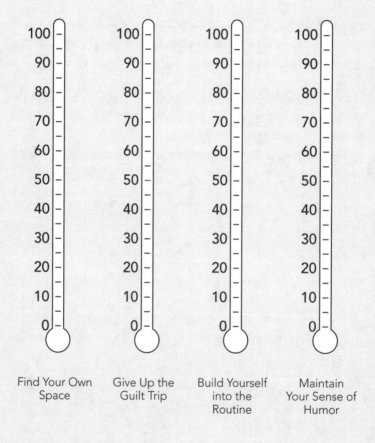

Find Your Own Space   Give Up the Guilt Trip   Build Yourself into the Routine   Maintain Your Sense of Humor

Of the four qualities, which one do you think is most important to work on right now in your life? Describe in specific terms one action you can take this week to do just that:

Time to Talk #3

Once you have completed this section, review it with your husband. Here are a couple of questions to guide your conversation, questions you can pose to him and discuss:

1. Do you agree that these are important things for me to do? Why or why not? Which one do you feel is most important (and least important) for me to do? Why?
2. Knowing that it's ultimately up to me, what is one practical and specific way that you can help me practice this kind of self-care?

You can answer the same questions for him once he completes his exercise in his workbook.

You may want to jot a note or two on your discussion here:

FOR GROUP OR
COUPLE DISCUSSION
WITH THE
ACCOMPANYING DVD

PART FOUR

Contents

Introduction to Your Small Group Study *111*

Session One: *How Your Personality Shapes Your Marriage* . *113*

Session Two: *What's a "Love Style"?* *117*

Session Three: *The Four Love Styles* *121*

Session Four: *Putting Your Love Styles to Work For You* *125*

INTRODUCTION TO YOUR SMALL GROUP STUDY

STUDYING THIS MATERIAL in a small group with other couples is one of the best ways to make it stick — and have a lot of fun in the process. Each session of this small group study contains a video component featuring Les and Leslie Parrott as well as other creative elements.

After viewing the DVD, you will find discussion questions on the following pages that you can use in each of your four small group sessions. Don't get hung up on answering every question in order. Use the questions that work best for the personality of your group.

You will see that some of the sessions are based on more than one chapter from the book. Obviously, you are going to get more out of the discussion if you've read the pertinent chapters. But if you haven't read them, don't worry. You can still join in on the discussion, and you don't need to feel an ounce of guilt. The purpose is to enjoy the interaction and learn from it. You can read the chapters later if you wish. The one element that you will likely find most helpful in this experience is to take the online Love Style Assessment (at RealRelationships.com).

You'll also find that each of the sessions will rely on an exercise or two from this workbook. We've selected exercises that will not put anyone on the spot or force anyone to share information they don't want to. Of course, your group may elect to use other exercises from this workbook to discuss if you wish. That's up to you and your group.

A key ingredient to successful small group discussion is vulnerability. Typically, the more transparent you are, the more meaningful the experience will be. And the more open others will be as well. Vulnerability begets vulnerability. However, we caution you not to use this time to gripe about your partner in some way. Don't embarrass each other by dragging out dirty laundry you know would upset your partner. In other words, be genuine and vulnerable, but not at the expense of your partner's feelings.

Another key ingredient in these discussions is specificity. You'll gain much more out of this time when you use specific examples with each other. So with this in mind, we will remind you every so often to "be specific."

One more thing. Each of the four sessions begins with a question that is "just for fun"—a kind of icebreaker. These questions are designed to simply get the wheels turning and help you connect as you come together in your group.

So relax. Have fun. And learn all you can to put your personal Love Style to work for you.

SESSION ONE:
How Your Personality Shapes Your Marriage

THIS SESSION IS based on chapter 1 of *L.O.V.E.* However, reading this chapter before or after you participate in this session is optional.

Just for Fun (5 minutes)

Think about the first date the two of you ever went on with each other. Where did you go? What did you do? The video will set you up to consider and share with the group what kind of impression you were trying to make.

Video Notes (10 – 15 minutes)

Talking about You (30 minutes)

- What do you think about the idea that your personality stems from deep down in your own genetic code? Does this make sense to you? Why or why not?

- Can you describe a moment early in your marriage or even your dating relationship when you began to see your spouse without a particular personality "mask" on to disguise an unattractive trait? How about a time when one of your masks was revealed?

- Can you think of something in your own personality that affirms the idea that your natural temperament is powerful? What internal need or urge do you have to feel like you're at your best?

Talking through Your Workbook Exercise (10 minutes)

Within your small group, take time to complete the portion of exercise 1 ("Exploring Your Personality Masks") in your workbook to which the video directs you.

After you have completed the exercise, take a few minutes to compare notes as a couple and then come back together as a group and share what you have learned in doing this exercise.

Making Time Together as a Couple

Spend some time in the days ahead, just the two of you, completing the remaining portions of exercise 1. Also, spend some time this week, just the two of you, talking about your small group session. What did you learn from other couples in the discussion this week? Finally, review the content of chapter 1 in the book, if you are reading it together, and even if you aren't, identify the most important "takeaway" you gained from studying this topic this week.

SESSION TWO:
What's a "Love Style"?

THIS SESSION IS based on chapter 2 of *L.O.V.E.* However, reading this chapter before or after you participate in this session is optional.

Just for Fun (5 minutes)

Think about how you express love to each other when you are in front of other people. What level of physical affection are you comfortable with in public? The video will set you up to consider and share with the group how your personality shapes the ways you express love.

Video Notes (10 – 15 minutes)

Talking about You (30 minutes)

- What do you think of the idea of having a personal "Love Style"? Does it make sense to you? Why or why not?

- If someone were to observe you over the past seven days, what evidence would they find to conclude that you are either project-oriented or people-oriented? And how do you feel about landing in either of these camps? Do you see one as better than the other? Why?

- Are you more fast-paced or slow-paced? Would your spouse agree with your conclusion? Why or why not? Be specific.

- If you have not already taken the online assessment, which one of the four Love Styles do you resonate with most and why? Which one do you predict your spouse will identify with most and why?

Talking through Your Workbook Exercise (10 minutes)

Within your small group, take time to complete the portion of exercise 2 ("Pin-Pointing Your Love Style") in your workbook to which the video directs you.

After you have completed the exercise, take a few minutes to compare notes as a couple and then come back together as a group and share what you have learned in doing this exercise.

Making Time Together as a Couple

Spend some time in the days ahead, just the two of you, completing the remaining portions of exercise 2, and consider taking the online Love Style Assessment. Also, spend some time this week, just the two of you, talking about your small group session. What did you learn from other couples in the discussion this week? Finally, review the content of chapter 2 in the book if you are reading it together, and even if you aren't, identify the most important "takeaway" you gained from studying this topic this week.

SESSION THREE:
The Four Love Styles

THIS SESSION IS based on part 2 of *L.OV.E.* However, reading these chapters before or after you participate in this session is optional.

Just for Fun (5 minutes)

Think about what object in your home might represent your Love Style. What comes to mind? The video will set you up to consider and share with the group how this might convey fresh insight.

Video Notes (10 – 15 minutes)

Talking about You (30 minutes)

- How well does your highest category (of L.O.V. or E.) describe you? Give it a percentage ranking and explain why. Be specific. In other words, back up your ranking with a few specific examples. You may find the summary table in this workbook helpful in your discussion.

- As you consider how you are hardwired for love, what is one specific thing that your spouse could do to better love you? Why might it be difficult for him or her to do this?

- When it comes to how you can better love your spouse, what is one thing you've learned in this session about your spouse that you can immediately put into practice and how? Also, what recommendation did you pick up on for loving your spouse that will be most challenging for you and why?

Talking through Your Workbook Exercise (10 minutes)

Within your small group, take time to complete the exercises in part 2 of your workbook, which the video will direct you to. Complete the portions that pertain to you. After you have completed the exercise, take a few minutes to compare notes as a couple and then come back together as a group and share what you have learned in doing this exercise.

Spend some time the days ahead, just the two of you, completing the remaining portions of the exercise. Also, spend some time this week, just the two of you, talking about your small group session. You may want to review your online assessment results and complete some of the exercises that come with it. What did you learn from other couples in the discussion this week? Finally, review the content of part 2 in the book, if you are reading it together, and even if you aren't, identify the most important "takeaway" you gained from studying this topic this week.

SESSION FOUR:
Putting Your Love
Styles to Work for You

THIS SESSION IS based on part 3 of *L.OV.E.* However, reading these chapters before or after you participate in this session is optional.

Just for Fun (5 minutes)

If you had a chunk of money that had to be spent on your relationship in the next twenty-four hours—just for fun (no paying off bills!)—and the free time with each other to enjoy it, what would you do and how would you spend the money? The video will set you up to consider and share your thoughts with the group.

Video Notes (10 – 15 minutes)

Talking about You (30 minutes)

- What is it like being married to a spouse with your husband's particular Love Style? In other words, what are the benefits and what are the challenges of living with this particular style? Be specific.

- Now that you have a clearer understanding of what makes your spouse feel most loved, what is one thing you can do in the next day or so to do just that? And which of the suggestions in this chapter for doing so seem most challenging to you when it comes to loving your spouse? Why?

- When it comes to staying healthy with your spouse's Love Style, which suggestion in this session do you personally feel could benefit you the most? And how, in specific terms, can you begin putting it into practice?

Talking through Your Workbook Exercise (10 minutes)

Within your small group, take time to complete the exercises in part 3 of your workbook, which the video will direct you to. Complete the portions that pertain to you.

After you have completed the exercise, take a few minutes to compare notes as a couple and then come back together as a group and share what you have learned in doing this exercise.

Making Time Together as a Couple

Spend some time in the days ahead, just the two of you, completing the remaining portions of the exercise. Also, spend some time this week, just the two of you, talking about your small group session. You may, once again, want to review your online assessment results and complete more of the exercises that come with it. What did you learn from other couples in the discussion this week? Finally, review the content of part 3 in the book, if you are reading it together, and even if you aren't, identify the most important "take away" you gained from studying this topic this week.

We hope you've enjoyed your small group experience.
We'd love to hear from you.
To provide feedback and to learn about
additional small group kits with Les and Leslie Parrott,
like this one, visit www.RealRelationships.com.

APPENDIX A:
Comparing the Four Love Styles

	L Leader: The Take-Charge Spouse	**O** Optimist: The Encouraging Spouse	**V** Validator: The Devoted Spouse	**E** Evaluator: The Careful Spouse
Title	Leader: The Take-Charge Spouse	Optimist: The Encouraging Spouse	Validator: The Devoted Spouse	Evaluator: The Careful Spouse
Descriptor	Doer	Talker	Watcher	Thinker
Motivator	Power	Popularity	Peace	Perfection
Need	Control	Pleasure	Harmony	Excellence
Fear	Failure	Rejection	Conflict	Mediocrity
Satisfaction	Save Time	Win Approval	Gain Loyalty	Achieve Quality
Motto	If it's worth doing—do it now	If it's worth doing—make it fun	If it's worth doing—we'll do it together	If it's worth doing—it's worth doing right
At Best	Goal-oriented Focused Self-confident Visionary Hard working	Fun-loving Positive Persuasive Sociable Encouraging	Loyal Agreeable Thoughtful Tolerant Nurturing	Orderly Conscientious Scheduled Purposeful Factual
At Worst	Stubborn Insensitive Annoyed Hot-tempered Domineering	Avoids conflict Dramatic Off task Procrastinates Forgetful	Introverted Indecisive Resists change Unenthusiastic Pleaser	Obsessive Critical Moody Suspicious Rigid
Definition of Love	Being intentional and active about building our future together	Being attentive and giving each other affection and acceptance	Being reassured that we are on the same team	Being thorough, accurate, and true to our commitments and standards
Approach to Conflict	Let's find a quick solution.	Let's work together to solve this.	Let me think this through on my own first.	Let me consider this from every angle.
Perspective	"The glass is half full—as long as I maintain control of it."	"The glass is half full—and contains more than you think."	"The glass is half empty—but we'll manage together."	"The glass is half empty—and probably leaking."

APPENDIX B:
Exploring Your Online L.O.V.E. Styles Report
An Exercise Kit for Couples

Contents

*Introduction: Maximizing the Benefits
of Your L.O.V.E. Styles Report.* 133

Exercise 1: General Characteristics 134

Exercise 2: Your Primary Motivators 137

Exercise 3: The Unique Value You
    Add to Your Marriage. 140

Exercise 4: How You Like Your Spouse
    to Communicate with You 144

Exercise 5: How Conversations Can
    Break Down with You 146

Exercise 6: Areas for Improvement 149

Exercise 7: How Your Husband Sees You 151

Conclusion: Leveraging What You've Learned 153

INTRODUCTION: MAXIMIZING THE BENEFITS OF YOUR L.O.V.E. STYLES REPORT

THIS WORKBOOK IS designed to help you interact with your husband as well as ask important questions about who you are in the context of your marriage, based on your online report. Working through these questions alone and with your husband can give you added insights into your own strengths and how to leverage your differences.

How to Get the Most from This Workbook

Have your L.O.V.E. Styles Report in hand.

Commit to taking at least a half hour of uninterrupted time to go through these exercises. By investing the time it takes to sit through one television program, you can gain tremendous insights into your relationship.

We highly recommend that you share your report and your exercise process with your husband. Make it an interactive experience, with positive conversation and plenty of affirmation.

We're committed to providing outstanding tools and customer service to each person who takes our assessments. Let us know how we can help you!

Drs. Les and Leslie Parrott
RealRelationships.com

Exercise 1:
General Characteristics

The Goal: To grasp a "big picture" of the character traits that make up your personal Love Style.

Please turn to "Your Love Style Graph" in your report.

Any of the four dimensions above the midline on this graph are prominent for you. It's not unusual to have more than one. So what do you think? Are you surprised by anything on this diagram of your personal style? Why or why not?

Now turn to the "General Characteristics" section of your report.

After reading through these three paragraphs, how accurately do you think they describe you in general terms?

Not at all									Very well
1	2	3	4	5	6	7	8	9	0

If portions of this general description don't fit well with you, that's okay. Focus on what does a good job of describing you. However, before you move forward in this exercise, ask your husband to rate how accurately he thinks these paragraphs describe you. Have him use the same one-to-ten scale. If your husband sees it differently than you do, note that difference here:

Now, focus on the first paragraph. Choose two statements that describe you best, that cause you to nod your head in agreement and say to yourself, "That's me."

1. _____

2. _____

For each of the statements you noted above, write down (on the same line) a recent and specific example of how that statement is demonstrated in your life. Thinking of specific examples will clarify your thinking.

From paragraph two, choose two statements about yourself that you think your husband most appreciates in you.

1. _____

2. _____

Now ask your husband if you did a good job identifying these two statements. Have him rate the accuracy of this on a scale of one to ten. If the accuracy level, according to your husband, is below an 8, ask him to explain, and note the explanation here:

Are there ways in which you are "holding back" on some of your personal qualities in your marriage? (Example: "It says I'm expressive, but I don't always share my true feelings with my husband.") Identify one or two ways you "hold back" and explain why you think that might be the case.

1. _____

2. _____

After exploring the General Characteristics portion of your report, what makes you feel the best? Why?

What statement in this section makes you feel like you need to focus more attention on improving a particular quality within yourself—especially as it relates to your marriage? Why?

Recommendation: If you have completed this exercise on your own, we encourage you to schedule a few minutes with your husband over the next two days to talk about what you learned—and to gain feedback from him on the General Characteristics describing you.

Exercise 2:
Your Primary Motivators

The Goal: To pinpoint the specific and unique motivators that make up your personal Love Style.

Please turn to the "Your Primary Motivators" section of your report.

Motivation is all about finding an incentive for action. This section of your report identifies several potential motivators that are likely to fit your style. You'll find some on this list that offer more incentive than others. Identify the top four desires from this section that are most important to you.

1. _____

2. _____

3. _____

4. _____

In your marriage, what tends to motivate you the most? Be honest and draw from the items in this section if needed. Use specific examples.

Do you believe that your husband is aware of the areas that tend to motivate you?

While we're at it, do you believe that you are aware of the areas that tend to motivate your husband?

Note one of the most important motivators for your husband here:

As you consider your motivators, note one specific thing from this section of your report that you wish your husband would do more often. Be specific. Note how, when, and why this would motivate you.

Recommendation: If you have completed this exercise on your own, we encourage you to schedule a few minutes with your husband over the next two days to talk about what you learned—and to gain feedback from him on your motivators.

Exercise 3:
The Unique Value
You Add to Your Marriage

The Goal: To increase the level of awareness, for both you and your husband, of what your personal Love Style adds to your marriage.

Please turn to "The Unique Value You Add to Your Marriage" section of your report.

Everybody brings special contributions to their relationship—contributions that only they can make. You can think of these as the strengths you add to your marriage. As you explore the list of these strengths from this section, list four statements that best describe your contributions and note a specific example for each of how you do that in your marriage.

1. _____

2. _____

3. _____

4. _____

In your marriage, how aware do you feel your husband is of your strengths?

Not at all								Very well	
1	2	3	4	5	6	7	8	9	0

How aware are you of specific relational strengths your husband adds to your marriage? List a couple of them.

From your list of strengths in this section, what are two that you could "tap into" a little more often? In other words, which of these qualities are maybe lying a bit too dormant within you as a wife? Why?

1. _____

2. _____

Note one specific action you can take in the next forty-eight hours to put a dormant strength into practice for your husband. Note in concrete terms the likely time and place of this behavior.

Are there any items from the "Relationship Strengths" section of your report that are the same, or are "synonymous," with those on your husband's report? If so, list them below.

List the strengths that seem to be totally different, or "opposite," from those on your husband's report.

Now that you have identified the differences in your strengths, list two specific differences that cause the most conflict in your marriage (for example, "I'm outgoing and social, and my husband tends to be more reserved"):

1. _____

2. _____

When and where are these differences most likely to cause the greatest consternation in your relationship?

What is one practical solution you can both agree on to make these times work better for both of you?

Recommendation: If you have completed this exercise on your own, we encourage you to schedule a few minutes with your husband over the next two days to talk about what you learned—and to gain feedback from him.

Exercise 4:
How You Like Your Spouse to Communicate with You

The Goal: To identify the specific keys to your personal Love Style as they relate to enjoying better conversations.

Please turn to the "How You Like Your Spouse to Communicate with You" section of your report.

Communication is the lifeblood of your relationship. The level of overall satisfaction you have in your marriage correlates with how well you are communicating. So how well have the two of you been communicating over the past few days?

Not at all								Very well	
1	2	3	4	5	6	7	8	9	0

What can you do to help your husband understand and improve how to best communicate with you? The list in this section of your report is a great place to start. What is the most important key to communication (from this section) for your husband to apply when communicating with you? Why?

From the answer above, apply the item you selected to a specific example of how your husband could use this key in communicating with you. Make sure you frame the application positively (this is not a time to point fingers). Write your example here:

Identify two additional items from this list that are most important for your husband to keep in mind when communicating with you.

1. _____

2. _____

Now, note a specific time and place (for each) where you would like your husband to put this into practice with you.

Recommendation: If you have completed this exercise on your own, we encourage you to schedule a few minutes with your husband over the next two days to talk about what you learned—and to gain feedback from him.

Exercise 5:
How Conversations
Can Break Down with You

The Goal: To identify the roadblocks to healthy communication that are commonly related to your personal Love Style.

Please turn to the "How Conversations Can Break Down with You" section of your report.

The last exercise focused on what your husband can do, proactively, to improve conversations with you. This exercise focuses on helping your husband know what to avoid in conversations with you.

Before we get into that, however, let's see it from your husband's side. Most of us tend to expect our husband to communicate with us just like we converse with him. However, different Love Styles use different means of communicating. Understanding your husband's natural communication style is a powerful way to "join" or "connect" with him. How likely are you to validate the way your husband approaches a conversation?

Not at all									Very well
1	2	3	4	5	6	7	8	9	0

Why did you rate this as you did? And do you have an example that backs up your rating?

Use the list in this section of your report to identify for your husband the one thing that would be most important, from your perspective, to avoid when communicating with you. And, as always, explain why.

From the answer above, apply the item you selected to a specific example in a conversation with your husband. In other words, what's a concrete example of how your husband can head off a potential communication problem with you? Make sure you frame the application positively.

List the two most important statements for your husband to follow as he communicates with you on a daily basis.

1. _____

2. _____

Compare your statements with those on your husband's report. Identify similar statements and list them below:

Take three statements from the list of "How Conversations Can Break Down with You" and rewrite them in a "positive" way by removing the "don't." For example, the statement "Don't be demanding or domineering" can be changed to "Be patient and relaxed when sharing your thoughts." These can be used as goals for solid interaction between you and your husband.

1. _____

2. _____

3. _____

Recommendation: If you have completed this exercise on your own, we encourage you to schedule a few minutes with your husband over the next two days to talk about what you learned—and to gain feedback from him.

Exercise 6:
Areas for Improvement

The Goal: To zero in on how you can improve your personal Love Style as it relates to your husband.

Please turn to the "Areas for Improvement" section of your report.

This section of the report highlights what you might think of as factors hindering optimum interaction with your husband. You may notice that each of the items in this section is a strength of yours that has been pushed too far. Every strength, as the saying goes, is a double-edged sword.

Identify and list two statements that tend to reflect your interactions at home.

1. _____

2. _____

The statements above indicate at least two specific strengths that you are pushing to an extreme. List the corresponding strengths from your personal Love Style.

1. _____

2. _____

Turn these two factors that hinder your relationship into action items or goals to keep your strengths "in check" when you interact with your husband. In other words, what will you do, in specific terms, the next time you see one of these factors emerging within you?

1. _____

2. _____

Recommendation: If you have completed this exercise on your own, we encourage you to schedule a few minutes with your husband over the next two days to talk about what you learned—and to gain feedback from him.

Exercise 7:
How Your Husband Sees You

The Goal: To zero in on your self-perception of your personal Love Style as well as on your husband's perception of you.

Please turn to the "How Your Husband Sees You" section of your report.

Read and reflect on this information. The words listed under "self-perception" are words that you would likely use to describe yourself in a positive light. However, it is natural for us all to display a negative side. We all have days when we are not at our best.

Look at the words that your husband may sometimes use to describe you. Which of these perceptions (if any) do you agree with?

If your husband ever has any negative perceptions of you, which ones would be the most frequent? Why?

Which of these perceptions can be, or have been, roadblocks in your marriage relationship?

It can be quite a challenge to change a person's perception of us. It is possible, for sure, but it can take some time. What specific changes or adjustments can you make in these areas that can have a positive difference in your relationship with your husband?

Recommendation: If you have completed this exercise on your own, we encourage you to schedule a few minutes with your husband over the next two days to talk about what you learned—and to gain feedback from him.

CONCLUSION:
Leveraging What You've Learned

CONGRATULATIONS! WE HOPE you have gained many valuable insights as you have completed the exercises to go along with your L.O.V.E. Styles Report. What matters at this point, of course, is that the lessons learned stay with you.

The final page of your report contains one-word descriptors of your specific Love Style. In a way, it summarizes much of what you've been exploring about yourself. It may be a good reminder to keep handy over the next few days. Compare and contrast your summary page with your husband's. It will surely generate some interesting conversation and shed some clarifying light on your relationship.

In addition to this, however, we have one final suggestion: Once you and your husband have both completed your individual exercises (and hopefully explored them a bit together), schedule a date night. Put it on the calendar now to meet in two or three weeks with your reports and these completed exercises. Take just twenty minutes or so to review what you have learned. And discuss these three questions:

1. What's the greatest "takeaway" I gained from exploring my personal Love Style? Why?

2. What's the one quality within myself that I am committing to improve as a result of these exercises?

3. What's the one thing I will now be doing more of to better love my husband as a result of doing these exercises?

That's it. Meet up in a couple of weeks—after you've had some time for this to seep in a bit more—and answer these three simple questions.

And please let us know how things go. We love to hear from you. And visit us at our website for lots of free resources and additional helps.

With every good wish and prayer,

Drs. Les and Leslie Parrott
www.RealRelationships.com

About the Authors

Drs. Les and Leslie Parrott are founders and codirectors of the Center for Relationship Development at Seattle Pacific University (SPU), a groundbreaking program dedicated to teaching the basics of good relationships. Les Parrott is a professor of psychology at SPU, and Leslie is a marriage and family therapist at SPU. The Parrotts are authors of *Becoming Soul Mates, Your Time-Starved Marriage, Love Talk, The Parent You Want to Be*, and the Gold Medallion Award-winning *Saving Your Marriage Before It Starts*. The Parrotts have been featured on *Oprah, CBS This Morning*, CNN, and *The View*, and in *USA Today* and the *New York Times*. They are also frequent guest speakers and have written for a variety of magazines. The Parrotts' radio program, *Love Talk*, can be heard on stations throughout North America. Their website, RealRelationships.com, features more than one thousand free video-on-demand pieces answering relationship questions. Les and Leslie live in Seattle, Washington, with their two sons.

Love Talk

Speak Each Other's Language Like You Never Have Before

Drs. Les and Leslie Parrott

A breakthrough discovery in communication for transforming love relationships.

Over and over, couples consistently name "improved communication" as the greatest need in their relationships. *Love Talk*, by acclaimed relationship experts Drs. Les and Leslie Parrott, is a deep yet simple plan full of new insights that will revolutionize communication in love relationships.

In this no-nonsense book, "psychobabble" is translated into easy-to-understand language that clearly teaches you what you need to do — and not do — in order to speak each other's language like you never have before.

Love Talk includes:

- The Love Talk Indicator, a free personalized online assessment (a $30.00 value) to help you determine your unique talk style
- The Secret to Emotional Connection
- Charts and sample conversations
- The most important conversation you'll ever have
- A short course on Communication 101
- Appendix on Practical Help for the "Silent Partner"

Two softcover his and hers workbooks are full of lively exercises and enlightening self-tests that help couples apply what they are learning about communication directly to their relationships.

Hardcover, Jacketed: 978-0-310-24596-4

Also Available:

978-0-310-26214-5	Love Talk	Abridged Audio CD
978-0-310-26467-5	Love Talk Curriculum Kit	DVD
978-0-310-81047-6	Love Talk Starters	Mass Market
978-0-310-26212-1	Love Talk Workbook for Men	Softcover
978-0-310-26213-8	Love Talk Workbook for Women	Softcover

Trading Places

The Secret to the Marriage You Want

Drs. Les and Leslie Parrott

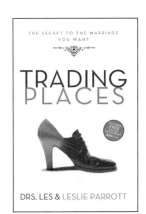

To understand your spouse you've got to walk in his or her shoes.

Ever feel like you're stepping on each other's toes? Then maybe it's time you put yourselves in each other's shoes. Of course that may sound uncomfortable. But it's easier than you think — and it will revolutionize your relationship. In fact, bestselling authors Drs. Les and Leslie Parrott reveal the little-known secrets of putting the time-tested strategy of trading places to work in your own marriage.

In this book, chock-full of practical helps and tips you've never thought of, you'll learn the three-step-strategy to trading places and, as a result, you're sure to:

- Increase your levels of passion
- Bolster your commitment
- Eliminate nagging
- Short-circuit conflict
- Double your laughter
- Forgive more quickly
- Talk more intimately

This book also features a powerful, free online assessment that instantly improves your inclination to trade places.

Most couples never discover the rewards of trading places. For example, did you know it's the quickest way to get your own needs met? It's true! And Les and Leslie show you how. They also disclose exactly how trading places improves your conversations and how it's guaranteed to fire up your sex life. Truly, your love life and your entire marriage will never be the same after you learn the intimate dance of trading places.

Softcover: 978-0-310-32779-0
Unabridged Audio CD: 978-0-310-28674-5

The Complete Guide to Marriage Mentoring

Connecting Couples to Build Better Marriages

Drs. Les and Leslie Parrott

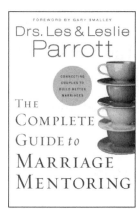

A comprehensive resource to help churches build a thriving marriage mentoring program.

Les and Leslie Parrott are passionate about how marriage mentoring can transform couples, families, and entire congregations. *The Complete Guide to Marriage Mentoring* includes life-changing insights and essential skills for

- Preparing engaged and newlywed couples
- Maximizing marriages from good to great
- Repairing marriages in distress

Practical guidelines help mentors and couples work together as a team, agree on outcomes, and develop skills for the marriage mentoring process. Appendixes offer a wealth of additional resources and tools. An exhaustive resource for marriage mentorship in any church setting, this guide also includes insights from interviews with church leaders and marriage mentors from around the country.

> "The time is ripe for marriage mentoring, and this book is exactly what we need."
>
> — Gary Smalley, author of *The DNA of Relationships*

Hardcover, Printed: 978-0-310-27046-1

Also Available:

ISBN	Title	Format
978-0-310-27047-8	51 Creative Ideas for Marriage Mentors	Softcover
978-0-310-27110-9	Complete Resource Kit for Marriage Mentoring, The	Curriculum Kit
978-0-310-27165-9	Marriage Mentor Training Manual for Husbands	Softcover
978-0-310-27125-3	Marriage Mentor Training Manual for Wives	Softcover

Pick up a copy today at your favorite bookstore!

ZONDERVAN®
.com

Saving Your Marriage Before It Starts

Seven Questions to Ask Before — and After —You Marry

Drs. Les and Leslie Parrott

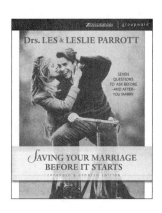

A trusted marriage resource for engaged and newlywed couples is now expanded and updated.

With more than 500,000 copies in print, *Saving Your Marriage Before It Starts* has become the gold standard for helping today's engaged and newlywed couples build a solid foundation for lifelong love.

This expanded and updated edition of *Saving Your Marriage Before It Starts* has been honed by ten years of feedback, professional experience, research, and insight, making this tried-and-true resource better than ever. Specifically designed to meet the needs of today's couples, this book equips readers for a lifelong marriage before it even starts.

The men's and women's workbooks include self-tests and exercises sure to bring about personal insight and help you apply what you learn. The seven-session DVD features the Parrotts' lively presentation as well as real-life couples, making this a tool you can use "right out of the box." Two additional sessions for second marriages are also included. The unabridged audio CD is read by the authors.

The Curriculum Kit includes a DVD with the Leader's Guide, hardcover book, workbooks for men and women, and *Saving Your Second Marriage Before It Starts* workbooks for men and women. All components, except for the DVD, are also sold separately.

Curriculum Kit: 978-0-310-27180-2

Also Available:

978-0-310-26210-7	Saving Your Marriage Before It Starts	Unabridged Audio CD
978-0-310-26565-8	Saving Your Marriage Before It Starts Workbook for Men	Softcover
978-0-310-26564-1	Saving Your Marriage Before It Starts Workbook for Women	Softcover
978-0-310-27585-5	Saving Your Second Marriage Before It Starts Workbook for Women	Softcover
978-0-310-27584-8	Saving Your Second Marriage Before It Starts Workbook for Men	Softcover

Share Your Thoughts

With the Author: Your comments will be forwarded to the author when you send them to *zauthor@zondervan.com*.

With Zondervan: Submit your review of this book by writing to *zreview@zondervan.com*.

Free Online Resources at
www.zondervan.com

Zondervan AuthorTracker: Be notified whenever your favorite authors publish new books, go on tour, or post an update about what's happening in their lives at www.zondervan.com/authortracker.

Daily Bible Verses and Devotions: Enrich your life with daily Bible verses or devotions that help you start every morning focused on God. Visit www.zondervan.com/newsletters.

Free Email Publications: Sign up for newsletters on Christian living, academic resources, church ministry, fiction, children's resources, and more. Visit www.zondervan.com/newsletters.

Zondervan Bible Search: Find and compare Bible passages in a variety of translations at www.zondervanbiblesearch.com.

Other Benefits: Register yourself to receive online benefits like coupons and special offers, or to participate in research.